Meeting the Needs of Second Language Learners

An Educator's Guide

Judith Lessow-Hurley

Association for Supervision and Curriculum Developn

D1166511

®

Association for Supervision and Curriculum Development
1703 N. Beauregard St. • Alexandria, VA 22311-1714 USA
Telephone: 800-933-2723 or 703-578-9600 • Fax: 703-575-5400
Web site: http://www.ascd.org • E-mail: member@ascd.org

All Web links in this book are correct as of the publication date below but
may have become inactive or otherwise modified since that time. If you
notice a deactivated or changed link, please e-mail books@ascd.org with the
words "Link Update" in the subject line. In your message, please specify the
Web link, the book title, and the page number on which the link appears.

Printed in the United States of America.

S3/2003

ISBN: 0-87120-759-1 ASCD product no.: 102043

ASCD member price: $13.95   nonmember price: $16.95

Library of Congress Cataloging-in-Publication Data
Lessow-Hurley, Judith.
    Meeting the needs of second language learners : an educator's guide /
Judith Lessow-Hurley.
        p. cm.
Includes bibliographical references and index.
    ISBN 0-87120-759-1 (alk. paper)
    1. Language and languages—Study and teaching—United States. 2.
Second language acquisition. 3. Bilingualism—United States. 4.
English language—Study and teaching—Foreign speakers. I. Title.

P51 .L498 2003
418'.0071'073—dc21

                                                        2002154697

12 11 10 09 08 07 06 05   12 11 10 9 8 7 6 5 4 3

Meeting the Needs of Second Language Learners

1

Who Is the Second Language Learner?

Fueled by immigration, the number of children in the nation's public schools has been increasing steadily over the last 20 years and is also becoming increasingly diverse (Jamieson, Curry, & Martinez, 1999). Newcomers to the United States tend to be younger than highly assimilated traditional populations, so schools have felt the impact of population changes in the latter part of the 20th century and the beginning of the 21st more rapidly and more dramatically than other social and government institutions.

It is difficult to estimate the number of English Language Learners (ELLs) or students who need assistance with English because different states use different tools to measure language proficiency. Recent data from the Office of English Language Acquisition (OELA) of the U.S. Department of Education (2001) indicate that nationwide in the 1999–2000 school year approximately 4.4 million schoolchildren K–12 were designated as ELLs. The number of second language learners in the public schools has grown substantially over time. OELA indicates that the number of ELLs has grown by nearly 105% since 1989 (see Figure 1.1). California currently reports nearly 1.5 million ELLs, or approximately one-fourth of its K–12 public school enrollment (California State Department of Education, 2000). That's significant because California's school enrollment represents 10 percent of all the nation's schoolchildren. Other states reporting large numbers of second language learners include Texas, with approximately half a million ELLs; Florida, with about 300,000; and New York, with approximately 250,000 students who lack English proficiency. Although those states top the list for numbers of ELL students, second language learners can be found in almost every part of the country. Every teacher in the United States must work toward the special understandings, skills, and dispositions needed to facilitate the language and academic development of students for whom English is a new language.

Basic Definitions

There is often confusion about the terms used to describe students who speak a language other than English. Some of this confusion is rooted in the fact that many terms overlap, and that some terms may even mean the same thing. This section defines commonly used terms such as *language minority* and *limited English* and analyzes language proficiency and the challenge of assessing it.

FIGURE 1.1

English Language Learners in the United States: A Growing Population

Year	Total K–12 Enrollment	Growth Since 1989	LEP Enrollment	Growth Since 1989
1989–1990	38,125,896	—	2,154,781	—
1990–1991	42,533,764	11.56%	2,232,500	3.61%
1991–1992	43,134,517	13.14%	2,430,712	12.81%
1992–1993	44,444,939	16.57%	2,735,952	26.97%
1993–1994	45,443,389	19.19%	3,037,922	40.99%
1994–1995	47,745,835	25.23%	3,184,696	47.80%
1995–1996	47,582,665	24.80%	3,228,799	49.84%
1996–1997	46,375,422	21.64%	3,452,073	60.21%
1997–1998	46,023,969	20.72%	3,470,268	61.05%
1998–1999	46,153,266	21.05%	3,540,673	64.32%
1999–2000	47,356,089	24.21%	4,416,580	104.97%

Data from National Clearinghouse for English language Acquisition & Language Instruction Educational Programs, *The Growing Numbers of Limited English Proficient Students, 2002.*

Language Minority Students

School districts often begin the process of figuring out which students will need help learning English by identifying language minority students. Language minority students are those who have a language other than English in their home background. A language minority student may come from a home where English is rarely or never spoken. Or a language minority student may share a household with a parent or a grandparent who speaks a language other than English.

One common practice for identifying language minority students is to send a language survey to newly enrolled students' parents or guardians, asking them about language use in their homes. If a language other than English is spoken in a student's home, that student may be considered "language minority." Language minority students are usually then tested for English proficiency. Language proficiency testing determines whether a language minority student is a monolingual English speaker, bilingual, or limited English proficient.

English Language Learners or Limited English Proficient Students

A *limited English proficient* (LEP) student is a student who by some measure, usually a standardized proficiency test, has insufficient English to succeed academically in an English-only classroom. Note that the term "limited English proficient" has provoked some controversy in the field because it is based on a deficiency model, labeling students by what they can't, rather than what they can, do. Some educators, therefore, prefer the term *English Language Learner* (ELL). Whichever term you use, it's important to remember that LEP/ELL students will need assistance with both English language development and content instruction in order to progress in school.

What Is Language Proficiency?

One of the difficulties in identifying students with limited English proficiency is the lack of agreement among theorists on a definition of proficiency. At a minimum, theorists tend to agree that the ability to use a language is related to the context in which it is used.

For example, if you have studied French extensively in college, you may be capable of writing essays in French on topics related to literature or philosophy. Stepping off a plane in Orly, however, you may find your French insufficient to the demands of changing money, finding a bus to Paris, or registering at your hotel. It's not that you don't know any French, but that you are weaker in some language skills than others.

Conversely, you may have been born in the United States and consider yourself a native Spanish speaker. In the absence of academic support for your native language, however, you may not have strong Spanish literacy skills. Your

ability to use Spanish is perfectly adequate for the requirements of daily life, such as shopping, phone calls, and social
events, but you might have difficulty making a professional
presentation or writing a research paper in Spanish.

The shortage of bilingual and biliterate speakers of
Spanish in the United States has had an effect on the avail-
ability of qualified teachers to staff bilingual classrooms
(Fern, 1998). Native-born Spanish-speaking teachers who are
not biliterate cannot themselves offer a fully enriched literacy program to their Spanish-speaking students. This self-
replicating problem results from an apparent ambivalence in
our civic conversation about American multilingualism and
our ongoing inability to formulate sensible educational and
language policies.

Language Proficiency and Schooling

Schooling appears to require particular kinds of language
proficiency because school is a highly specialized context.
Cummins (1981) has clarified the issues of language proficiency and context for educators. He suggests that school-
related tasks require school-related proficiency, which he has
labeled Cognitive Academic Language Proficiency (CALP).
According to Cummins, CALP is the kind of language we use
in situations that don't have a lot of context-related clues.
CALP is different from what Cummins calls Basic
Interpersonal Communicative Skills (BICS), the kind of
language we use for day-to-day communication. In ordinary

daily communication we can often extract meaning from the situation or context, which gives us lots of clues.

For example, you can generally get something to eat or shop for souvenirs in a foreign country even if you don't speak the language. Shopping and eating in restaurants are contexts that are comparable from place to place. When you go into a restaurant and look at the menu, or enter a store and look at the merchandise, everyone understands what you have in mind. In addition, you can use gestures and facial expressions to communicate. You can also make your needs known with a few simple words like "please" and "thank you." Shopping and eating in restaurants are activities that relate to concrete visible objects and events; they are based on shared assumptions and scripts. That is to say, they are highly contextualized. It is easy to understand and be understood in highly contextualized situations, even if you have limited language skills, or BICS.

On the other hand, it is difficult even for fairly competent speakers of a second language to follow a university lecture about abstract ideas. In a lecture, there is little to give you a real sense of the topic or to clarify what's going on. An instructor may provide a lecture outline or make notes on the board or projection screen, but print is, by definition, extremely abstract. University lectures are decontextualized. That is to say, few communication clues exist in the lecture context. Attending a university lecture requires a particular set of highly sophisticated academic language skills, or CALP.

Even early primary classrooms are decontextualized. It's certainly feasible for a kindergarten teacher to make a lesson about the weather a concrete, hands-on experience. Children can go outside and stand in the rain or feel the warmth of the sun. And mathematics manipulatives can provide direct experience with numbers. But schooling becomes increasingly less contextualized as it becomes more advanced. Although upper primary and secondary teachers may be skilled at providing hands-on experiences across the curriculum, at higher grades much of what is taught relies on listening, reading, and writing.

And finally, what appears simple and straightforward to an adult may be abstract and difficult for a youngster. The demands of 3rd grade may not seem as challenging as those of a university class, but 3rd grade is (and should be) challenging for a 3rd grader. Put yourself in the shoes of a 3rd grader with limited English skills trying to participate in a social studies lesson. For instance, imagine yourself in a university classroom in Beijing or Cairo trying to take notes on a history or political science lecture in preparation for an examination or a research paper.

In sum, academic experiences and activities at every level are generally more abstract and lacking in context than day-to-day, real-life communication, so they present difficulties for students who have not developed academic language skills, or CALP. And commonly used proficiency tests do not always assess CALP. As a result, children who have playground English are often judged as English proficient even though they may not be able to handle the demands of schooling in their new language. Failure to distinguish between contexts unfairly sets up those students for failure.

Cultural Diversity in the Public Schools

Linguistic diversity is one simple indicator of the unprecedented cultural diversity in our public schools. But even as classrooms diversify, public school teachers tend to be overwhelmingly white and middle class. And though very few Americans can claim indigenous roots, teachers are most often from highly assimilated backgrounds characterized by mainstream values and mores. In fact, many Americans, teachers included, are so mainstream that they describe themselves as "Heinz 57" and claim to have "no culture." That notion, however, is based on an erroneous idea of what culture really means.

What Is Culture and Who Has It?

Human beings are cultural by their very nature. We engage our world through the manufacture of artifacts, the practice of behaviors, and the development and adherence to values and beliefs. We share our culture with others in our groups and communicate our culture to our children in an ever-evolving response to the circumstances and challenges of our worlds. We don't all have the same culture, and we don't all share the same degree of relationship with our heritage or ethnic cultures, but we all have culture.

Culture is what human beings believe, think, make, and

do to adapt to their environments. Bullivant (1993) posits three basic environments to which we all adapt: physical, social, and metaphysical. Bullivant's notion is best understood by exploring a simple example such as housing. All human beings create dwelling spaces, but not all of them do it the same way. The physical environment has a direct impact on how people design and build houses. For example, peaked roofs are useful where it snows, and masonry houses aren't practical where there are earthquakes.

But beyond the physical demands of the environment, houses respond to and reflect social environments. Americans usually have "family rooms," as well as living rooms. Family rooms are more casual, usually contain a television, and get far more use than living rooms, which are considered formal. Older homes in the United States don't have family rooms, but may have big eat-in "farm" kitchens. When heating a home was difficult or central heating was unavailable, congregating in a warm kitchen made sense. This harks back to the physical environment, but most certainly shaped and was shaped by family dynamics as well. All our environments interact and overlap.

The social dimensions of housing are complex. Wealthy people often live in big houses in desirable locations. But no matter how much money you have, you can't call a realtor and make an offer on the White House, even though it may be smaller than some of the houses in the affluent part of your town!

The response to a metaphysical environment may be harder to discern than responses to physical and social environments, but such adaptations are no less real. Realtors in areas with large populations of Asian immigrants often keep lists of houses that oblige the principles of *feng shui*, a metaphysical system that considers the placement of houses and the configuration of interiors and furnishings essential to good fortune. For example, houses with front doors that open to face staircases are considered unlucky, as are houses on T-intersections. Orthodox Jews may have two kitchen sinks, one for meat products and another for milk products, in keeping with the requirements of *kashruth*, a metaphysical system that requires, among other things, the separation of meat from dairy.

And almost all of us, regardless of our ethnic or religious heritage, take pride in the look of our houses and do things simply to beautify our homes. To place a flower arrangement on a table, hang a painting, or choose a colorful rug all engage us in aesthetics, which is a response to the metaphysical environment.

Multicultural Education

The need to respond to children from many different cultural backgrounds has led some educators to express a need for multicultural education. Multicultural education, however, has been interpreted in a variety of ways. The weakest and probably the least effective approach to multiculturalism is the scatter-shot insertion of holidays and celebrations related to various ethnic groups into the curriculum. This might entail a celebration on Cinco de Mayo or recognition of contributions of African Americans during Black History Week. Multicultural educators sometimes refer to this approach as "tacos and chitlins," or "display window" multiculturalism.

Of course, nothing is wrong with including attention to personalities and holidays in the curriculum. But culture is more than feasts and celebrations. Strong multicultural education implies the reform of schools in such a way that schooling can facilitate the academic success of students from all backgrounds (Banks, 1993). And the strongest versions of multicultural education suggest that students be prepared to identify issues and challenges in their own environments related to social justice, and that they learn the skills needed to effect societal change (Howard, 1999). This is easy to say, but difficult to do. Historically, schooling in the United States has generally supported the status quo and assimilation of newcomers and traditional minorities into mainstream culture.

The scope of this book does not allow an exploration of the dimensions and tensions of multicultural education. The key issue for educators is to understand that schooling is more than the 3 Rs—schools are brokers between home cultures, school culture, and all the cultures of the larger world. Schools need to be reflective of and responsive to the histories, values, and beliefs of students from a variety of backgrounds. And teachers need to examine their unstated and often unacknowledged assumptions and carefully consider the purposes and outcomes of schooling. Only then will schools be able to serve students from diverse backgrounds well.

References

Banks, J. A. (1993). Multicultural education: Characteristics and goals. In J. A. Banks & C. M. Banks (Eds.), *Multicultural education: Issues and perspectives* (2nd ed., pp. 3–28). Boston: Allyn and Bacon.

Bullivant, B. M. (1993). Culture: Its nature and meaning for educators. In J. A. Banks & C. M. Banks (Eds.), *Multicultural education: Issues and perspectives* (2nd ed., pp. 29–47). Boston: Allyn and Bacon.

California State Department of Education (2000). *Limited English proficient students and enrollment in California public schools, 1993 through 2000.* Sacramento, CA: Author.

Cummins, J. (1981). The role of primary language development in promoting success for limited English proficient students. In *Schooling and language minority students: A theoretical framework.* Los Angeles: Evaluation, Dissemination, and Assessment Center, California State University, LA.

Fern, V. (1998, July). *What is the impact of biliteracy/bilingualism on the economy?* Washington, DC: National Clearinghouse for Bilingual Education.

Howard, G. R. (1999). *We can't teach what we don't know: White teachers, multiracial schools.* New York: Teachers College Press.

Jamieson, A., Curry, A., and Martinez, G. (1999). *Social and economic characteristics of students* (U.S. Census Bureau Publication No. P20-S33). Washington, DC: U.S. Department of Commerce, Economics and Statistics Administration.

National Clearinghouse for English Language Acquisition & Language Instruction Educational Programs. *The growing numbers of limited English proficient students.* Washington, DC: U.S. Department of Education.

▲   ▲   ▲

Read More About . . .

➤ The number and distribution of second language learners at www.ncbe.gwu.edu, the Web site for National Clearinghouse for English Language Acquisition and Language Instruction Educational Programs (NCELA), formerly known as the National Clearinghouse for Bilingual Education. This site is a rich resource for information about services to second language learners. Current information about demographics and policies is available on a state-by-state basis.

➤ Language proficiency testing in the *Handbook of English Proficiency Tests* by Ann del Vecchio and Michael Guerrero (Evaluation Assistance Center, Western Region, New Mexico Highlands University, Albuquerque, 1995). The handbook provides an overview of issues related to language proficiency testing and describes five frequently used tests, from both theoretical and practical perspectives.

➤ The distinction between cognitive and academic language proficiency and basic interpersonal communication skills in *Schooling and Language Minority Students: A Theoretical Framework*, edited by the California State Department of Education, Office of Bilingual Bicultural Education (Los Angeles, CSU-LA Evaluation, Dissemination, and Assessment Center, 1981). In particular, see the chapter by Jim Cummins, "The Role of Primary Language Development in Promoting Academic Success for Language Minority Students." Cummins's theoretical framework has become part of the language educators speak when they are discussing language proficiency, and as a result this chapter can be seen as current and relevant despite its publication date.

▲   ▲   ▲

2

WHAT EDUCATORS NEED TO KNOW ABOUT LANGUAGE

THE PRESSING DEMANDS OF SCHOOLING LARGE NUMBERS OF SECOND language students often outweigh theoretical considerations. As a result, simplistic notions of language and language development are all too often at the heart of both the politics and programs for students who don't speak English. Without an informed idea of the nature of language, it is impossible to structure useful educational approaches for second language learners. This chapter explores several important dimensions of language and language development and their implications for teaching.

What Is a Language?

It's not surprising that we sometimes refer to our first language as a "mother tongue." Language is far more than a means for labeling objects and ideas in the world around us. We learn our language from the people around us as we learn the world. Our language is an encoding system for the complex network of meanings that make up our experience. Whether you believe, as some theorists do, that language shapes the way we perceive the world, or as others propose, that the world shapes the language we use, it is inarguable that our perceptions of reality and our language are inextricably linked.

Language Communicates

The primary purpose of language is communication. Therefore, despite common misperceptions, mastery of a language does not require near-native pronunciation or grammar. What theorists call *communicative competence* is far more important than a good accent or perfectly constructed sentences. If you are learning a language and you can understand and can be understood when you speak, you are well on your way.

Although there is certainly value to learning a language in conformity with the norms of native pronunciation and usage, sophisticated usage and graceful expression come only with practice and use. With a focus on communication, nativelike proficiency is not the goal of language teaching, but rather a happy by-product of the basic need that people have to communicate with each other.

Language Is Systematic

Language communicates with words—arbitrary symbols systematically organized to convey meaning. In spoken languages, words are made up of sounds. Every language selects a limited array of sounds from all the possible sounds humans can make and uses that particular selection for its phonological system—the sounds used to convey meaning. For example, Spanish makes a distinction between a simple *r* that sounds a lot like an English *d,* as in "caro" (expensive), and a rolled *rr* as in "carro" (cart or car). "Caro" and "carro" sound similar or even identical to English speakers, because English does not distinguish between the two sounds. The difference is clear to Spanish speakers because the Spanish phonological system uses the distinction to convey meaning.

Languages also systematically order parts of words, such as prefixes, suffixes, and roots, in a system called *morphology.* In English, "cats" has two morphemes, one that describes an animal (cat), and another that asserts plurality (s). And words are systematically arranged in sentences in a system called *syntax.* The sentence "The chorp butled harfily in the turgle" has no apparent meaning, but a morphological analysis tells an English speaker that there was only one chorp, that it performed an action in the past, that the action was performed with harf, and that the whole event happened in the turgle. You can figure all that out from the architecture of the words and the sentence because they follow a standard English system. The sentence may not make sense in the real world, but it makes sense linguistically!

The sounds and architecture of a language are relatively easy to discern. Often less transparent is the system of meanings, or *semantics*. Beware the person who cheerfully announces that any argument you are making is "just semantics." Semantics is precisely where the linguistic rubber hits the road. As an English speaker you know that someone telling you to "knock it off" isn't asking you to remove the cherry from your ice cream sundae. Or as Mark Twain once said, "The difference between the right word and the almost right word is the difference between lightning and a lightning bug." It's not surprising that treaties, trade agreements, business contracts, and even office e-mails are often closely edited. In the final analysis, words carry big, important packages of meaning, and, whether we say so or not, we know that semantics cannot be trivialized or ignored.

Language Varieties

All languages vary depending on where they are spoken. If you have traveled in the United States, you have probably encountered varieties of English different from your own. People in different parts of the country have different accents, use different words for familiar objects, and structure their sentences differently. This is true for every language, even in relatively small places. Languages also vary depending on who's speaking them. For example, schoolteachers usually sound different from taxi cab drivers when they speak. Men and women often use different social dialects and speak differently to members of the opposite sex than they do to their own.

We all speak some variety of our own language, and we all vary our speech depending on the situation—what we are talking about, to whom, and why. But we tend to assume that other people have a dialect and we have none, and we also tend to assume that other people's language varieties are imperfect or not "proper." It is true that some varieties of language are less socially or politically acceptable than others, but they are all communicative, systematic, and appropriate for use in their own communities.

Our judgments about language acceptability are tied to deep social and political values. For example, in the United States, black dialects are generally less acceptable than white dialects, even white dialects that deviate noticeably from standard English. This is not a judgment about language. Rather it is a reflection of the dynamics of race in American social and political history.

Bilingualism

Bilingualism is difficult to define. Monolinguals tend to think that bilinguals use two languages equally well for all purposes. In fact, bilinguals may have an uneven repertoire of language skills. In the United States, for example, many people speak Spanish proficiently for everyday purposes but, having never been schooled in Spanish, are not biliterate. Inversely, people for whom Spanish is not a home language may study it in a traditional school setting, become reasonably literate, but never develop communicative competence. For example, they may not master the intricacies of fast-moving, casual conversation or the subtleties of social obligation and courtesy.

In an environment where two languages are socially available, bilinguals often switch back and forth between them. Teachers sometimes assume that students who code-switch lack proficiency in either language. This is usually not the case. Code-switching is not a primitive survival skill for the linguistically deprived. To the contrary, code-switching is a sophisticated way to use two languages in a bilingual setting to communicative advantage. For example, people code-switch to repeat and emphasize a point: "I told him and told him. Le dije. But he just wouldn't listen!" Code-switching may be used to communicate intimacy: "Listen, m'hijo [my son, with endearment], you need to clean up your room. Vienen tus primos [your cousins are coming]."

Also, when languages come into contact with each other, they naturally borrow useful words and structures. In the United States, English and Spanish are in vital contact with each other. The result is lots of "Spanglish." The term is usually used pejoratively, but that's a political dimension of a linguistic inevitability. When English speakers use the word "taco" they don't think much about it, but it's a Spanish word. It can be translated (a deep fried unleavened tortilla? . . . crepe? . . . pancake? filled with ground beef and salad, and served with salsa? . . . sauce?), but why bother? English is rich and complex because it has borrowed freely from the many languages with which it has had contact over centuries.

Similarly, Spanish speakers in the United States adopt words and phrases from the English that surrounds them. In one American Spanish dialect "Te wacho" means "I'll see you around." And you've probably heard English speakers say "no problema." It's not standard Spanish, but it's commonplace; and everyone seems to agree that it's "no problema" at all.

Implications for Educators

Language communicates, and does so systematically. Without analyzing the details of any language teaching methodology, a focus on those two ideas may well alter how you look at language teaching and learning. Although we all ultimately want students to develop their new language to the fullest possible extent, what we know about the nature of language should lead us to think carefully about how we go about meeting that goal.

Teachers, being teachers, are fond of correctness. As a result, teachers rely all too often on repetition, memorization, and especially correction when instead they should create situations that motivate children to communicate. Consider what constant correction does to communication: If someone corrected your speech every time you spoke, what would the effect be? How long before you gave up trying to talk altogether?

Although the inner works of each system vary from language to language, all language is inherently systematic. So people learning a new language think systematically, and often may make language judgments based on what they already know. The rules they apply may not work in their new language, but the judgments show that they are on to something. Errors made by second language learners often constitute a window of opportunity for teachers to use for assessment and instruction.

Languages vary across time, space, and social class. Some varieties are considered standard, and one of the tasks of schooling is to bring all children into the world of standard speech and writing, regardless of their social or linguistic background. But the language and language variety that each child speaks is useful in that child's speech community, and should not be treated with distaste or disrespect. Teachers who acknowledge and value their students' home language build students' self-esteem, a powerful foundation for learning.

Finally, language is tied to deep identity. When you speak a language you participate in its culture. It may not be a conscious goal, but schools often try to replace home languages with English even though there is no need to forget a language to learn a new one. Whatever your political position, it needs to be understood that language replacement implies cultural replacement as well. This is not a trivial matter, and one that educators must understand as they embark on meeting the needs of second language learners.

Language Learning

It is generally assumed that we will teach language effectively if we understand how language is learned. That's easy to say, but difficult to do. Some language learning processes can be explained through brain research. Neurolinguists have made progress on identifying the areas of the brain that process language, often collecting data from cases where stroke or trauma victims have experienced language difficulty, loss, and even unusual recall. Recently, in an effort to separate language functions from auditory functions, neurolinguists have begun to study the development of sign language (Hickok, Bellugi, & Klima, 2001).

But most language learning seems to be a function of the mind, a far more elusive subject for research than the brain. Psycholinguists' data is limited to their subjects' output, often gathered in case studies of young children as they learn first and subsequent languages.

In the latter part of the 20th century, freed from earlier assumptions that bilingualism was a handicap, researchers developed useful theories about language acquisition that can guide educators as we all meet the needs of second language learners in school.

Learning a First Language

Young children acquire their native language (or languages) with remarkable speed, facility, and depth, and the study of how they accomplish that goes back to ancient times. Until well into the 20th century, it was generally believed that memorization was the main factor in language learning—that babies listened to and memorized what they heard around them in association with what was going on at the time. The flaw in that argument is simple. If we only were able to say what we had already heard, we would never be able to say anything that hadn't been said before!

In the mid-20th century, Noam Chomsky, a renowned linguist, suggested that human beings had a predisposition to learn a language, which he called the language acquisition device (LAD) (1971). The LAD was activated by input children received from the adults and caregivers around them. In contemporary terms, the computer provides a useful analogy to Chomsky's concept. A computer is preprogrammed to receive software that you install. The operating system is like the LAD, and software is like a particular language.

Based on more recent research, theorists now believe that babies need more than a stream of unmoderated input to learn a language. Babies need interaction, and the input they receive in interaction with caregivers is carefully organized to help them develop language. Adults engage in strategies to help babies learn: speaking slowly and carefully with lots of repetition, referring to concrete objects, engaging in naming rituals, and filling in where youngsters may not yet have words for concepts they are trying to express.

And children engage in strategies to keep caregivers in the interaction, not the least of which is simply being cute.

Doctors who do voluntary plastic surgery in underdeveloped nations around the world usually fix a cleft lip before they fix a cleft palate when a two-step procedure is mandated. Babies who can't smile are at a terrible disadvantage—people tend to ignore or shy away from them.

Note that adults and children don't use these strategies consciously. They don't need textbooks or professional development workshops. Humans have a deep need to communicate, and language is a primary vehicle for enculturation. So from the time children are born, we all support, scaffold, and encourage their ability to speak.

Children move through stages of language development, and the stages are universal around the world. Babies cry, then coo, then babble. When they babble, they seem to be using the sounds of their native language to the exclusion of others, and theorists think they may be practicing the sounds that make up the phonological system of their mother tongue. Remember that when you try to learn or teach a new language. Adults often have difficulty with the accent of a new language, but that shouldn't be surprising when you consider how early you learn the phonological habits of your own.

Children build the rule systems of their language, trying out lots of general ideas and learning exceptions as they go. So small children may say "mouse" and "mice," but then switch to "mouse" and "mouses" because they have figured out the way plurals work. Later on they get more sophisticated, and "mice" reappears in their speech. They may generalize about concepts, calling all animals "doggie," even when they can identify different animals in pictures or at the zoo. Children speak child versions of their language, which evolve and grow as they develop and broaden their understandings of language and the world.

Learning a Second Language

As with first language development, it is impossible to "see" language acquisition processes at work, and researchers must base their work on the available data, that is to say, the language that learners produce. Unlike first languages, second languages are learned with varying success. For example, it is generally assumed that young children learn language better than adults. Although that is arguable—because adults frequently learn new languages for a variety of reasons—it is clear that youngsters are more apt to acquire a new language without an accent.

The reasons for this variability are difficult to discern. For example, researchers have tried to identify the effects of age on second language acquisition, but that is only one of several outside variables that may affect the process (Gass & Selinker, 1994). Personality also seems to affect a person's ability to learn a new language—people who are outgoing and willing to take risks are likelier to master a new language than those who aren't. But perhaps that personality quality is related to age—children seem far more willing than adults to act playful or silly and to accept the inevitable pratfalls that come with play.

Motivation is also a factor in learning a new language. For example, adults may choose to learn a new language to advance in a job. Children are less likely to understand economic motivation, but early work by psycholinguist Lily Wong Fillmore (1979) suggests that the desire to make friends motivates children, and that friendship scaffolds their language acquisition. Wong Fillmore's work suggests that teachers create classroom environments that support social interaction, using strategies such as buddies, pair shares, and cooperative grouping.

Stephen Krashen's popular theory of second language acquisition (1994) suggests that language is best acquired informally rather than learned in traditional school settings with traditional methodologies. Krashen suggests that traditional language teaching encourages the use of a "monitor," a set of rules that constrains us from freely entering into interaction. Krashen's monitor hypothesis would explain why adults are more hesitant to use a new language than children: Unlike children, adults are likely to know there are rules and want to use them. As a result, adults are inhibited from diving in and making the best of an interaction, which, according to Krashen's theory, is exactly where the most effective language acquisition occurs.

Implications for Teaching

Particulars of second language acquisition theory should lead teachers to think about creating warm, welcoming classroom environments and using strategies that motivate students to communicate with each other, rather than using repetitive drills or grammar exercises. And teachers should remember that the difference between learning a second language and learning a first is less about language or process, and more about the learner. Second language learners have knowledge of a language and, through that language, substantial knowledge of the world. If learning a new language is seen as problem-solving, second language learners come equipped with tools that can help. This leads us, paradoxically, to consider the value of first language development, especially in the early grades. It may seem counter-intuitive, but broadening children's experience of the world and developing their base of skills and concepts in their first language, strengthens their ability to engage a new language (see Chapter 3).

References

Chomsky, N. (1971). Language acquisition. In J.P.B. Allen & P. Van Buren (Eds.), *Chomsky: Selected readings* (pp. 127–148). London: Oxford University Press.

Gass, S. M. & Selinker, L. (1994). *Second language acquisition: An introductory course*. Hillsdale, NJ: L. Erlbaum.

Hickok, G., Bellugi, U. & Klima, E. S. (2001, June). Sign language in the brain. *Scientific American*, 57–65.

Krashen, S. (1994). Bilingual education and second language theory. In C. F. Leyba (Ed.), *Schooling and language minority students: A theoretical framework*. Los Angeles: Evaluation, Dissemination, and Assessment Center, California State University, LA.

Wong Fillmore, L. (1979). Individual differences in second language acquisition. In D. Bennett Durkin (Ed.), *Language issues: Readings for teachers*. New York: Longman.

▲   ▲   ▲

Read More About . . .

➤ Language varieties in a short and entertaining article by sociolinguist Walt Wolfram, "Everyone Has an Accent," in *Teaching Tolerance Magazine* (Number 18, Fall 2000). Dr. Wolfram appears in *American Tongues*, produced by Louis Alvarez and Andrew Kolker (Center for New American Media, 1987), a lively documentary about dialect in the United States. The interviews, dramatizations, and observations support an excellent explanation of language variety, with engaging examples recorded across the United States. *Dialects in Schools and Communities* by Walt Wolfram, Carolyn Temple Adger, and Donna Christian (L. Erlbaum, 1999) provides an in-depth scholarly treatment of language variety and the implications of dialect for instruction. *The Power of Babel,* by John McWhorter (Times Books, 2001) is an excellent overview of ideas about language variety. The discussion is sufficiently detailed to inform the professional reader, and also informed with the author's lively and entertaining personal anecdotes and reflections.

➤ Black English, sometimes called Black Vernacular or Ebonics (a variety of English that excites a great deal of discussion and controversy), in *The Real Ebonics Debate: Power, Language and the Education of African-American Children* (1998). Edited by Theresa Perry and Lisa Delpit, and published by Rethinking Schools and Beacon Press, it contains James Baldwin's powerful essay, "If Black English Isn't a Language, Then Tell Me, What Is?"

➤ The way men and women use language in *You Just Don't Understand* by Deborah Tannen (New York: Morrow, 1990). This book is one of the many popular and scholarly books that Tannen has written about social uses of language in general and gender discourse in particular.

➤ Second language acquisition in *Second Language Acquisition: An Introductory Course* by Susan M. Gass and Larry Selinker (L. Erlbaum, 1994). This text provides an excellent overview of the nature of language, describes research methodologies in second language research, and explores in some depth the factors that affect second language acquisition.

➤ The history of the Roman alphabet, literacy, and the ancient world, all wonderfully intertwined in *Alpha Beta: How 26 Letters Shaped the Western World* (New York: Wiley, 2000).

➤ How the Internet has affected language in *Language and the Internet* by David Crystal (New York: Cambridge University Press, 2001). Anyone who sends e-mail or surfs the Web will find something of interest in this book, which is both scholarly and accessible.

3

BEST PRACTICES

HOW BEST TO MEET THE NEEDS OF SECOND LANGUAGE LEARNERS IN the public schools has persistently bogged down in political debate, which often takes place with little reference to theoretical issues, research findings, or the real day-to-day challenges that face both students and teachers. Proponents of bilingual education insist that students for whom English is not a first language are best served with some form of primary language instruction, and strong arguments exist to support that contention. Proponents of English-only education, who insist that those students are best served with immediate and intensive exposure to English, often sway the general public.

Both *English language development* (ELD)—often called *English as a Second Language* (ESL)—teachers and bilingual teachers serve the same group of students and know that there are many different approaches to meeting their students' needs, depending on those students' first language development as well as their social and personal contexts for learning. For young students and those who speak no English at all, first language instruction is usually desirable; and in those cases, appropriate English language development is also a key program component. In some settings, first language development may not be feasible, and good ELD programs can go a long way to assist youngsters with the challenges of school.

This chapter describes the benefits of primary language instruction for second language learners and provides an overview of bilingual program models and English language development strategies.

Working with ELL Students in Their Primary Language

Few people, when questioned directly, deny the value of knowing two languages. "I studied French in high school," people sigh, "and now I can't speak a word. I really wish I could speak a second language." Given the prevalence of that attitude, it's surprising that many people object to bilingual education and resist the idea of using languages other than English in public school classrooms. "Why should I use my tax dollars," the argument goes, "to teach these kids a foreign language? They should learn English as quickly as possible, and we should expose them to as much

English as we can." The resistance to bilingual education in public schools is not resistance to an education in two languages but to instruction in minority languages for language minority children.

Fueled by political appeals that feed on the fear of the effects of increased immigration, many states have passed English-only laws, and several have outlawed bilingual education altogether. California, for example, passed a proposition in 1998 mandating that all instruction be offered "overwhelmingly" in English. The argument against the use of primary language instruction sounds powerful and has strong intuitive appeal, but it breaks down under careful scrutiny. Contrary to popular belief, research indicates that primary language instruction in the classroom actually helps students learn English and fosters academic success:

➤ Concepts and skills that students learn in one language transfer to another. Time spent learning in a language other than English is not time wasted. In fact, for many children, time spent in their primary language is time gained on academic tasks. This is particularly true for small children, who have not fully grasped basic concepts.

Ramirez, in a large-scale study funded by the federal government (1992), compared the academic performance of students in a variety of programs, including programs where students were immersed in English, those where they had some primary language support in early grades only, and those where primary language support was continued through late primary grades. Even though students in English immersion and "early-exit" programs progressed academically at the same *rate* as their English-speaking peers, they never caught up with their peers academically. Students in programs that continued primary language instruction through the late elementary school years caught up academically with the general population.

More recently Collier and Thomas (2002) published findings from a five-year study that analyzed achievement data from more than 200,000 students in five school districts. They note, "English language learners immersed in the English mainstream because their parents refused bilingual/ESL services showed large decreases in reading and math achievement by Grade 5" (p. 2).

The conclusions of these large-scale studies are hardly surprising if you think about a child who doesn't have proficiency in English and enters kindergarten in an English-only classroom. By the end of the year, the child will most likely have developed some command of English. But while that child is deciphering the language code, all the other children are learning the kindergarten curriculum. In a primary language instruction setting, ELL students can learn age- and grade-appropriate skills and concepts without falling behind their English-speaking peers.

➤ Strong primary language development helps students learn English. At first, this may appear illogical, but in fact, it makes good sense: Students who understand how their native language works can transfer their understanding to the study of English. According to one study, LEP students who entered ESL programs between the ages of 8 and 11 learned English faster than LEP students who entered ESL programs between the ages of 5 and 7 (Collier, 1987). Cognitive and linguistic maturity seems to give older students an advantage over younger ones, who have a limited understanding of the workings of the world and their language. The issue here is not nativelike proficiency, but the speed of acquisition, a key factor in school success.

➤ School-related tasks require a fairly sophisticated grasp of language. Even after ELL students can manage day-to-day situations in a new language, they may experience difficulty in meeting the academic expectations of an English-only classroom (Thomas and Collier, 1997). Depending on many factors, including age, birthplace, home country school experiences, and age on arrival in the United States, students may need anywhere up to ten years to develop the language skills needed for academic tasks, or cognitive academic language proficiency (CALP) (Garcia, 2000). Primary language instruction gives students time to develop their language and also their all-important literacy skills, without losing valuable academic ground.

➤ Students who are highly proficient in two languages appear to have academic advantages over monolingual students. Classroom instruction revolves around language. Cummins (2000) reviewed studies that show that in a variety of social and linguistic contexts, bilingual students who have access to more than one language code appear to have the academic advantage of highly developed metalinguistic and problem-solving skills not only in language but also in mathematics. And not surprisingly, students who have proficiency in two languages acquire a third with more ease than students who don't. Cummins concludes, "the continued development of academic proficiency in bilinguals' two languages is associated with enhanced metalinguistic, academic, and cognitive functioning. (p. 182)"

➤ Supporting primary language bolsters self-esteem. Language is an inseparable part of an individual's personal and cultural identity. To the extent that the school validates a child's language (and by extension, culture), that child will feel valued in the classroom (Baker, 1988). In addition, support for community languages transmits a welcoming message to parents and encourages them to become involved in their children's education (Miller, 1990).

Additive versus Subtractive Bilingualism

We can begin to resolve the debate over the value of primary language instruction by considering the difference between additive and subtractive bilingualism.

A *subtractive bilingual* is a person who has replaced a first language with a new one; the first language is undeveloped, or lost. Students become subtractive bilinguals in the absence of formal schooling in their primary language. Such students may maintain oral proficiency in their first language, but they don't enjoy the benefits of language and literacy development for that language. Compared with additive bilinguals, subtractive bilinguals are at an academic disadvantage.

An *additive bilingual* is a person who has learned a second language in addition to a native language. Monolingual English-speaking students become additive bilinguals when they acquire a second language—often in expensive private school settings where bilingualism is valued as an essential component of a good education! LEP students can become additive bilinguals in programs that maintain their first language and add English as a second language. Additive bilinguals seem to have an academic advantage over subtractive bilinguals and monolinguals.

The difference between additive and subtractive bilingualism has important implications for educational policy and practice. The value of additive bilingualism should lead educators to consider providing both second language instruction for students who speak only English and primary language instruction for students whose native language is not English.

Program Models

Bilingual education, most simply defined, is an instructional program that uses two languages. This definition is an oversimplification, but it is useful for clearing away confusion and political tension. A more in-depth understanding requires an analysis of instructional programs. How are two languages used? For whom? And to what end?

Transitional Programs

Probably the most common form of bilingual education in the United States today, *transitional* programs are the least controversial because the goal of a transitional program is to make students monolingual and monoliterate in English. In transitional programs, primary language is generally used to assist students with their academic work for a short period of time, usually through second or third grade. When students have gained proficiency in English, they enter English-only classrooms.

ELL students in transitional programs have more success in school than those who have had no primary language support. But students are often exited from transitional programs before they have fully developed their academic English skills, and they have difficulty with schoolwork in the years that follow. Also, transitional programs are not additive and do not have the benefits of programs that develop a child's first language as well as English, sometimes called *maintenance* programs.

Immersion Programs

The term *immersion* is often misunderstood and misused. Traditional immersion programs, modeled on programs originally developed in Canada, are enrichment programs that provide dual language instruction for native English speakers. Immersion programs use the students' new language as the medium of instruction. They are bilingual programs because of the following characteristics:

➤ The teacher is bilingual. Although the teacher delivers instruction in a language that is new to the students, students can express themselves and be understood in their own language.

➤ The language used for instruction is carefully modified and mediated to improve student understanding. All instruction is supported by the use of visuals, media, and hands-on experiences.

➤ Students usually receive language arts instruction in their primary language.

Immersion for ELL Students

The success of traditional immersion programs in Canada and more recently in the United States has led policymakers to consider placing ELL students in English immersion settings. Even when such programs are staffed with bilingual teachers, they tend to be less successful than traditional programs in promoting bilingualism and biliteracy. Immersion programs seem to work best when speakers of a majority language are immersed in a minority language. This is because majority language speakers are in no danger of losing their primary language, which is supported not only by language arts in a true immersion program, but also by society as a whole. In other words, immersion programs, like others, work best when their emphasis is additive.

As the result of recent legislation that has led to a move away from primary language instruction in many states, ELL students are often placed in English-only classrooms. This is

sometimes described as placing them in immersion programs. This is a misuse of the term "immersion." Placing students in classrooms where they cannot be understood and
where the instruction is incomprehensible has been more
appropriately called *sink-or-swim* or *submersion.*

Two-Way Immersion Programs

The traditional immersion model has generally been pro-
moted as enrichment for English-speaking students who
want to learn a second language. Such programs are particularly effective for that group of students, in large measure for
sociolinguistic reasons. The last 20 years have seen increased
interest in two-way immersion programs, which serve both
ELL and English monolingual students. According to a
recent report (Howard & Sugarman, 2001), currently 253
two-way immersion programs in 23 states and the District of
Columbia offer instruction in Spanish, Chinese, French,
Korean, or Navajo.

In *two-way immersion* programs, all instruction is delivered in a language other than English. Classes are mixed and
include both monolingual English speakers and speakers of
the language of instruction. Programs vary, but generally
monolingual English speakers receive English language arts
for part of each day while ELL students receive English language development.

As students advance through the grades, the amount of
English language arts and ELD instruction increases. At

about 3rd grade, two things occur: (1) ELD instruction begins to approximate English language arts as ELL students develop their English skills into literacy; and (2) the program is expanded to include the delivery of some subjects in English. The instructional goal is to create a classroom where half the instruction is delivered in English and half in another language, usually by 4th or 5th grade.

As in traditional immersion, the teacher is bilingual; however, in two-way immersion, she delivers all instruction in the language other than English. Instruction is carefully modified and mediated for comprehensibility. And unlike traditional programs, English speakers rely on the assistance of their peers, many of whom usually have some English and serve as translators when needed. English speakers are not silenced because they can express themselves and be understood. Minority language speakers develop their primary language, and at the same time are motivated to use their English to help their friends. And both groups have significant interaction with native speakers of the language that is new for them.

All students receive the same instructional program, except for the content of early English language development. Within that program, students have the following experiences:

➤ ELL students have an additive maintenance experience. That is to say, they add English while continuing the development of their home language.

➤ Monolingual English speakers have an additive enrichment experience. They learn a new language at no expense to the development of their English.

Results of longitudinal studies on two-way immersion (Lindholm-Leary, 2000) indicate that these programs are successful in promoting bilingualism and biliteracy as well as high levels of academic achievement. Students also report satisfaction with school and indicate in many cases that they stayed in school because of the program. In addition, students have positive attitudes toward people with backgrounds and languages different from their own—an extremely important outcome in a multicultural society and an increasingly interdependent world.

Working with ELL Students in English— English Language Development

Research indicates that primary language instruction supports (1) academic success by allowing students to stay abreast of the curriculum while learning a new language and (2) learning a new language by providing a strong language foundation for English language development. Primary language support may not, however, be available for a number of reasons. Under present legislation, some states are enjoined from providing primary language instruction. At a more practical level, where there is only a small population of speakers of a given language, it may not be feasible to create a classroom, much less a multigrade program, or to find a bilingual teacher to staff one. Either as a feature of a bilingual program or as a freestanding instructional approach, English language development is essential.

Traditional Approaches

Approaches and methods in second language teaching have changed rapidly in the last 50 years as assumptions about learning in general and second language learning in particular have evolved. Until World War II, languages were usually taught as they had been for centuries, using the *grammar-translation* approach, which emphasizes grammatical analysis and pencil-and-paper exercises. Those of us who experienced this approach can probably remember many tedious hours of learning conjugations and declensions, but little, if anything, about the living language we were studying.

World War II created a dramatic need for military personnel proficient in a great variety of languages, many of them quite exotic from the American perspective, and some of which had no writing system at all. In response to that need, and in keeping with the behaviorist model of learning that was popular at the time, the military developed what has come to be known as the *audio-lingual* approach to second or foreign language instruction. The audio-lingual approach assumes that we learn language by making it a habit. The method, therefore, emphasizes repetitive, structured oral drills and dialogues focused on language patterns. Oral communication is the priority, and reading and writing are added for advanced students.

The audio-lingual approach as implemented in military settings also included follow-up conversations and activities with native speakers of the target language. Despite the fact that our understandings of language learning have evolved, many classroom teachers still rely on pattern drills like those of the audio-lingual approach. They usually do not, however, supplement the drills with opportunities for the natural conversation that was likely a key factor in the success of the original approach.

Language Through Content

Based on recent theory about how second language is acquired—which assumes that language is best learned when meaningful messages are communicated in comfortable, nonthreatening settings—new approaches to language teaching often tie language to content.

Planning for Second Language Instruction

Tying language to content requires careful planning. As with all instruction, teachers first have to identify key content-related objectives. Then, based on an assessment of students' language abilities, they must also identify language objectives that are absolutely necessary for the content they have chosen. For example, students may need specialized vocabulary for a particular lesson in science or social studies. Or they may need help with academic language such as "compare and contrast" or "estimate." Finally, teachers will want to consider language objectives that may not be absolutely required by the content but are compatible with it. These types of objectives can serve as a way of expanding students' language skills. For example, a science lesson might lend itself to the language of prediction: "What would happen if . . . ?" or "What will happen when . . . ?"

Cooperative Grouping

Interaction is key to language development. A recent study (Sharkey & Layzer, 2000) showed that ELL students are often blocked from succeeding academically because they are placed in low-tracked classrooms, on the assumption that they can't handle challenging work in English. Those classrooms, unfortunately, tend to rely heavily on individual work and question-answer formats rather than collaborative, interactive work. Also, teachers in low-track classes spend time managing student behavior, and second language learners are often overlooked. The net result is that ELL students are denied precisely the kind of exchange of meaningful, motivating messages that they need to build their second language skills.

Cooperative learning is a particularly useful strategy for promoting interaction, increasing and upgrading the amount of student-initiated talk in the classroom. Because it creates situations where students must exchange useful information and communicate with each other, it is a useful strategy for supporting second language learners in both content learning and language development.

Sheltered Instruction

In a *sheltered* approach, teachers modify and mediate instruction to make content comprehensible to students learning in a second language. Sheltering requires that teachers modify their language to facilitate understanding. They slow down their speech, use repetition and synonyms, and avoid highly idiomatic usage. Instruction is mediated through visual aids and hands-on activities that enhance comprehensible input. Thematic instruction is useful for sheltering content, because it provides opportunities for students to take what they have learned in one area of the curriculum and use it in another.

Sharkey and Layzer (2000) found that teachers had low expectations of second language learners, and they expressed the idea that "trying" constituted success for their ELL students. Garcia (1997) cites an earlier study by Tikunoff (1983), who found that successful teachers of ELL students communicated high expectations to their students. Garcia's subsequent case study of three successful elementary school teachers reinforced Tikunoff's assertion. According to Garcia (p. 370), "These teachers portrayed themselves as quite demanding: they take no excuses from students for not accomplishing assigned work and they are willing to be 'tough' on those students who are 'messing around.'" Effective sheltered teachers do not "dumb down" content, but hold high expectations for their students, create a context for instruction, and enhance meaning so as to support second language learners.

References

Baker, C. (1988). *Key issues in bilingualism and bilingual education.* Clevedon, England: Multilingual Matters.

Collier, V. P. (1987). Age and rate of acquisition of second language for academic purposes. *TESOL Quarterly,* 21(4), 617–641.

Collier, V. P., & Thomas, W. P. (2002). *National study of school effectiveness for language: minority students' long-term academic achievement: Executive summary.* Santa Cruz, CA: Center for Research on Education, Diversity and Excellence.

Cummins, J. (2000). *Language, power, and pedagogy: Bilingual children in the crossfire.* Buffalo, NY: Multilingual Matters.

Garcia, E. E. (1997). Effective instruction for language minority students: The teacher. In A. Darder, R. D. Torres, & H. Gutierrez (Eds.), *Latinos and education: A critical reader* (pp. 362–372). New York: Routledge.

Garcia, G. N. (September, 2000). *Lessons from research: What is the length of time it takes limited English proficient students to acquire English and succeed in an all-English classroom?* (Issue Brief No. 5) Washington, DC: National Clearinghouse for Bilingual Education.

Howard, E. R., & Sugarman, J. (2001). *Directory of two-way immersion programs in the United States.* Washington, DC: Center for Applied Linguistics.

Lindholm-Leary, K. (2000). *Biliteracy for a global society: An idea book on dual language education.* Washington, DC: National Clearinghouse for Bilingual Education.

Miller, J. M. (October 31, 1990). Native-language instruction found to aid L.E.P.'s. *Education Week,* 10(9), 1, 23.

Ramirez, J. D. (1992). Executive summary. *Bilingual Research Journal,* 16 (182), 1–62.

Sharkey, J., & Layzer, C. (2000). Whose definition of success? Identifying factors that affect English language learners' access to academic success and resources. *TESOL Quarterly,* 34(2), 352–368.

Thomas, W. P., & Collier, V. (1997). *School effectiveness for language minority students.* (NCBE Resource Collection Series, No. 9.) Washington, DC: National Clearinghouse for Bilingual Education.

Tikunoff, W. J. (1983). *Compatibility of the SBIF features with other research on instruction of LEP students.* San Francisco: Fair West Laboratory.

▲ ▲ ▲

Read More About . . .

➤ Two-way immersion programs in *Biliteracy for a Global Society: An Idea Book on Dual Language Education,* by Kathryn Lindholm-Leary (National Clearinghouse for Bilingual Education, 2000). This short publication provides an excellent overview of the key features of two-way immersion programs. For a detailed discussion, see Lindholm-Leary's book, *Dual Language Education* (Multilingual Matters, 2001), which presents findings based on analysis of data for 8,000 students at 20 schools. Also, the Center for Applied Linguistics (CAL) is an excellent resource for information about two-way immersion, including frequently asked questions, a searchable directory of programs, and a list of publications (www.cal.org/pubs/twoway_p.html).

➤ A rationale for bilingual education in *Under Attack: The Case Against Bilingual Education,* by Stephen Krashen (Culver City, CA: Language Education Associates, 1996). Also, see *Myths and Realities: Best Practices for Language Minority Students,* by Katharine Davies Samway and Denise McKeon (Heinemann, 1999).

➤ Bilingual program models, described in *The Foundations of Dual Language Instruction,* by Judith Lessow-Hurley (Longman, 2000).

➤ The challenges faced in secondary schools in *Overlooked and Underserved: Immigrant Students in U.S. Secondary Schools* by Jorge Ruiz-de-Velasco, Michael Fix, and Beatriz Chu Clewell (2000). Structural constraints such as departmentalized classes and the complexity of high school schedules, combined with inadequate staffing and the unique needs of young adults, present serious challenges for high schools. This recent report, published by the Urban Institute, details those challenges and makes recommendations for policy and reform that address them.

▲ ▲ ▲

4

TEACHER QUALIFICATIONS

FEW PEOPLE WOULD SUGGEST THAT ALL ENGLISH SPEAKERS OR EVEN all English-speaking teachers have the ability to teach English. All too often, however, lay people and even some professionals assume that any English-speaking teacher can teach English as a second language, and any teacher who speaks two languages is a bilingual teacher.

Simply knowing the target language or languages, however, is not enough. Professional organizations as well as state licensure agencies recognize that teachers need specialized competencies to work effectively with second language learners. According to a recent survey (National Clearinghouse for Bilingual Education, 1999), 36 states and the District of Columbia offer ESL teacher certification, and 23 of those states require that certification for teachers placed in ESL classrooms. The same survey says that 23 states offer bilingual certification, and 17 of those require that teachers placed in bilingual classrooms hold that certification. Beyond language, what qualifies teachers who work with second language learners?

The Bilingual Teacher

Teacher licensure, because it is governed by the states, is inconsistent from one state to another in many regards, and bilingual teacher certification is no exception. Of the 23 states that offer bilingual teacher certification, 5 mandate courses or course content; 1 mandates a set of electives; 7 mandate a set of competencies that may be demonstrated by examination; and 6 mandate some combination of courses, electives, and demonstrated abilities (Menken & Antunez, 2001). The remaining 4 states did not specify dates or requirements.

Despite the variety of means to achieve the end, general agreement exists among the states and in professional organizations about the areas of knowledge, skill, and disposition that constitute competency in meeting the needs of second language learners. Most professionals agree that teachers of second language learners need awareness, skills, and knowledge related to language, pedagogy, culture, and community relations.

Teachers' Language Skills

All teachers of second language learners need in-depth knowledge about how language is structured, how it varies, and how children develop their first language and acquire additional ones. Whether or not they speak their students' home languages, they need to value the language that their students bring to the classroom.

Bilingual teachers need a high level of proficiency in their students' home language. State education agencies that offer bilingual certification usually determine teachers' second language ability by testing. Although the measures vary from place to place, the common expectation is that bilingual teachers will be able to use English and the target language for all social and professional purposes, including listening, speaking, reading, and writing. Ideally a bilingual teacher is a balanced bilingual, a person who can understand, speak, read and write two languages with equal proficiency, at the level of an educated speaker of either.

Language proficiency for teachers, as for others, must be viewed in the context of the situations they encounter. Bilingual teachers, like all teachers, deliver instruction. To do so, they should be competent in standard varieties of both English and the target language of their classrooms, and they should be capable of delivering instruction in required skill and content areas in both languages. Teachers do more than teach, however. To put it another way, teaching involves more than the delivery of instruction.

Consider the following situation: School has been in session for almost a month when Rocío comes to kindergarten. Newly arrived from Mexico, she speaks no English and is overwhelmed and bewildered by her circumstances. Rocío cries for most of her first day at school, and her mother, worried about leaving her, sits in the back of the room.

On the following day, the teacher tactfully asks Rocío's mother to leave. It takes Rocío about 20 minutes to calm down, and she remains tearful all day, requiring frequent attention and comfort. This continues for three days, until Rocío begins to feel comfortable in her new environment.

This situation is familiar to anyone who has taught kindergarten. It is presented here to illustrate that teachers often need to communicate with parents and children in emotional or difficult circumstances. This requires a situationally appropriate command of language quite different from the language skills necessary for instructional purposes. Bilingual teachers must be able to deliver instruction in a standard variety of both classroom languages, but they must also be able to communicate with students and parents in noninstructional contexts.

Beyond Language

Tests of teacher competency in the area of culture are often multiple-choice measures containing items related to names, dates, habits, and significant accomplishments of a particular group of people. Such lists and recipes, however, fail to respond to the real needs of children in classrooms. Consider the following incident: A Mexican American migrant farm work student is slightly injured during recess, and the teacher in charge takes her to the nurse. Several of her brothers and sisters crowd around and attempt to accompany her to the nurse's office. The office is small, and the nurse suggests that the children should return to the schoolyard.

Sensing the children's reluctance to leave, the teacher indicates that it would be best if they all stayed. The child's small scrape is quickly cleaned and bandaged as her siblings look on, and all the children return happily to play. The teacher understands that the children feel a strong sense of responsibility for their brothers and sisters, and that leaving their sister alone would make them uneasy. Small scrapes are a day-to-day reality on any playground, and this incident illustrates that teachers encounter cultural values at work in every facet of school life.

Professional educators generally agree that every teacher must develop specialized awareness, skills, and knowledge to work in culturally diverse settings. They agree less about what constitutes the culture knowledge base that teachers need to have. This is complicated by the fact that even linguistically homogenous classrooms may be culturally diverse. For example, Spanish speakers come to schools in the United States from many different parts of Mexico, Latin America, and the Caribbean. Their cultural backgrounds are very different.

No individual teacher can know everything there is to know about all the cultures in any classroom, or even about any single culture, including her own. And as the anecdote of the child injured in the playground illustrates, teachers must respond to the deep, *implicit* characteristics of culture, rather than the more superficial, *explicit* ones (Arvizu, Snyder, & Espinosa, 1980).

Working in a culturally diverse setting requires an understanding of the nature of culture, with an emphasis on value and belief systems. Skills in observing and analyzing cultures and an appreciation for diversity are essential to developing an understanding of culture in general and of specific cultures represented in a classroom. Finally, children in school experience the interaction of two cultures: their own and the culture of the school. Teachers need to develop the ability to avoid the potential pitfalls and to promote the positive outcomes of the intersection of home and school cultures.

Sociocultural Issues

Teaching and learning take place in a social and cultural context. Consider this situation: District policy has structured bilingual classrooms so that no more than half the children are ELL. The instructional rationale for this format is that fluent English speakers will provide models for second language learners. Several fluent English-speaking students, however, begin to tease the ELL students, particularly the newly arrived immigrants. The teasing is not well-intentioned and runs the gamut from remarks about personal appearance to exclusion from schoolyard games. Immigrant students, already overwhelmed by school, are becoming more withdrawn with each passing day. The teacher begins to implement a program that stresses positive interpersonal relations in the hope of improving classroom climate.

The cultural diversity of the United States presents a unique set of circumstances that must be considered in a discussion of teacher competencies. Some Americans are newly arrived; others can trace their ancestry back centuries. Except for the descendants of the indigenous peoples of the Americas, all Americans have roots elsewhere.

The United States has been compared on the one hand to a melting pot, and on the other to a salad bowl. The melting pot metaphor suggests that all cultures contribute ingredients to produce an amalgamated American. Salad-bowl ideology envisions each culture contributing its flavor and individuality to produce an appetizing mix. In either picture, the unique history of the United States and the resulting composition of American society produce contact among cultures, which may in turn produce conflict between people.

Teachers who work with diverse student populations must understand the dynamics of *enculturation,* which takes place when children learn the elements of their own culture, and of *acculturation,* when they learn the elements of a new one. Teachers must also understand the dynamics and tension of *assimilation*—what happens to people as they enter a new culture and elements of their own are altered or even eradicated. Teachers need to develop an understanding of the nature of culture conflict and be able to cultivate a positive cross-cultural classroom environment. This requires not only an awareness of the sociocultural dynamics, but knowledge and understanding of the history and contributions of minority cultures in the United States, and the ability to incorporate them into materials and activities.

Teacher Effectiveness

Program models and curricular approaches have been discussed in previous chapters, but teacher efficacy cannot be emphasized enough. Recent research has highlighted the positive effects of good teaching (Haycock, 1998). Regardless of children's socioeconomic status or language background, it is clear from current research that good teaching makes a difference for all children.

Early research on teacher efficacy found that effective teachers for second language learners have high expectations for their students, engage them actively in the subject matter, use both their students' languages, and value and incorporate aspects of home culture in schoolwork (Tikunoff, 1983). In a more recent case study (1997), García also found that effective teachers of second language learners use active, cooperative approaches to engage students and organize the curriculum so as to respond to and reflect students' culture. García identifies key dispositions of effective teachers, including dedication, confidence, and a lack of complacency. Effective teachers for second language learners reject what García calls the "pobrecito model" (p. 371), the idea that because the "poor little ones" come from unprivileged or difficult backgrounds they can't learn and should not be exposed to rigor. Effective teachers hold all their students to high standards.

References

Arvizu, S., Snyder, W. A., & Espinosa, P. T. (1980). *Demystifying the concept of culture: Theoretical and conceptual tools.* (Vol. III, no. 11.) Bilingual Education Paper Series. (pp. 362–372) Los Angeles: Evaluation, Dissemination, and Assessment Center, California State University, LA. New York: Routledge.

Garcia, E. E. (1997). Effective instruction for language minority students. In. A. Darder (Ed.), *Latinos and education.* New York: Routledge.

Haycock, K. (Summer, 1998). Good teaching matters: How well qualified teachers can close the gap. *Thinking K-16,* (3)2, pp. 1–2.

Menken, K., & Antunez, B. (2001). *An overview of the preparation and certification of teachers working with low English proficiency students.* Washington, DC: George Washington University, Center for the Study of Language and Education.

National Clearinghouse for Bilingual Education (1999). *Which states offer certification or endorsement in bilingual education or ESL?* Washington, DC: Author.

Tikunoff, W. J. (1983). Compatibility of the SBIF features with other research on instruction of LEP students. San Francisco: Far West Laboratory.

▲   ▲   ▲

Read More About . . .

➤ The qualities of good teachers for second language learners in the *English as a New Language: Standards,* published by the National Board for Professional Teaching Standards (1998). The National Board has created a system of certification for exemplary teachers that requires rigorous assessments based on standards devised by a wide variety of experts in various fields of pedagogy. The National Board standards for teachers of English as a new language represent a consensus of the field, and they offer a detailed description of the knowledge, skills, and dispositions that characterize an excellent teacher of second language learners. The worldwide professional association Teachers of English to Speakers of Other Languages (TESOL) has developed TESOL P-12 teacher standards, which organize the domains of language, culture, pedagogy, professionalism, and culture. More information is available at www.tesol.org.

➤ *The State Survey of Legislative Requirements for Educating Limited English Proficient Students,* by Andrew McKnight and Beth Antunez (1999) is available online and includes a state-by-state summary of teacher licensure. A table of teacher licensure options is linked to detailed information about each state's offerings and requirements. The report is available at www.ncbe.gwu.edu.

▲   ▲   ▲

5

LANGUAGE POLITICS, LANGUAGE POLICY, AND SCHOOLING

IF YOU PRESENT PRESERVICE OR EVEN FIRST-YEAR NOVICE TEACHERS with the idea that schools are political, they are often baffled and even somewhat uninterested. After all, their most pressing concern is what to do with the kids in class tomorrow. And though their focus on day-to-day classroom life is understandable, experienced educators know well that those classrooms are like small ships tossed on the much larger waves of politics at the district, state, national, and even international level.

From the outset the founding fathers of the new American republic envisioned public schools as essential tools for creating a population that could function in a participatory democracy. Although that is still a valuable and venerable purpose for public schooling, in today's increasingly complex world the purposes of schooling are not nearly so simple and clear. It has become more and more difficult to identify the apparently multiple purposes of schooling, much less gain consensus about them.

Everyone agrees that children are our most precious resource, that they should all have access to a good education, that they should achieve. But in a multiethnic, multidenominational, multilingual society with broad geographic, socioeconomic, and value spectra, what constitutes a good education, what children should achieve, and how they should achieve it, isn't at all clear.

In the United States, schools are the first place that most children experience a mandatory interaction with the government. That's a delicate interaction, because it is the exact place where parents have to relinquish some of their power to the state. That is not trivial, and the extent to which schools can assume parental power has, on more than one occasion, been debated all the way to the U.S. Supreme Court. At the local level, schools can become what Giroux (1988) has called "contested spheres" (p. 126). Giroux describes schools as places where some kinds of knowledge are validated and other kinds of knowledge are excluded. You know what he is talking about if you have ever been involved in the choice of textbooks, in a debate about phonics versus whole language reading methodologies, or a controversy about religious practice in public school classrooms.

If you doubt that schooling is political, consider that women were denied access to schools during the Taliban regime in Afghanistan; that Jewish children were legally expelled from school in Nazi Germany; that Paolo Freire, the great Brazilian educator, lived his life in exile for the crime of having effectively taught illiterate people to read by using materials and approaches the prevailing government perceived as threatening. Closer to home, consider that every recent president has wanted to be the "education president," that the governor in your state can change what you teach, and that your teachers' union can probably influence who will be governor and who will be president.

Teachers generally see themselves as caring advocates for students, as people who facilitate personal and professional growth for others, as people who give others access to necessary and desired skills. At their best, teachers are all of that and more. But they are also agents of the state. It may be the furthest thing from the mind of a new, first-year teacher, but it's important because teaching is always political.

Language Is Political

Languages are tied to cultures, ethnicities, and ultimately to personal identities. Where political agendas clash with cultural and personal agendas, conflict often results. For example, governments can and have outlawed the use of languages in attempts to subjugate groups of people that might threaten an established order. Recently, the Turkish government jailed 17 students who signed a petition asking their local university to offer an optional course in the Kurdish language (*Mercury News* Wire Services, 2002).

As the Kurdish students in Turkey are clearly aware, schools are often a primary instrument of government language policy. In the United States, for example, schools have been used to suppress Spanish and Native American languages, which were commonly outlawed or punished in public schools during the 19th and well into the 20th century. Carl Gorman, the father of the famous Native American artist R. C. Gorman, remembers being chained to a radiator for speaking Navajo in school (Thomas, R. M., Jr., 1998). Ironically, in World War II Carl Gorman served as a Navajo code talker. Code talkers helped the United States win the war by transmitting essential messages in a code based on the Navajo language.

Indigenous languages were not the only targets for language restrictionists in the United States. German was the target of an English-only movement that started early in the 19th century. Linked to anti-Catholicism and a fear of immigrants that's paradoxically almost as old as the nation itself, the movement grew following the American Civil War and then in the period leading up to World War I, when anti-German sentiment intensified. The use of German was outlawed in public places, and attempts were made to limit its use not only in public schools, but also in private schools and churches (Crawford, 1992).

Following the war, Nebraska tried unsuccessfully to prohibit the use of any foreign language in public schooling. The U.S. Supreme Court, in *Meyer v. Nebraska* (1923), overruled the state. It was a victory for German speakers, but German never regained the stature it once had—you can't resurrect schools, teachers, and curricula and eliminate deep-rooted fear and embarrassment with a stroke of the judicial pen.

The idea of language as a political force comes up in ordinary conversation when people assert the need to make English the official language of the United States. The underlying assumption is that multiple languages threaten our political unity. Incidentally, many people assume, without really thinking about it, that legislation that makes English an official language will automatically result in everyone speaking English. This is an erroneous assumption.

An official language is a language that people can use to interact with the government for purposes such as schooling, voting, or using public health facilities or the court system. Some countries, like Switzerland, recognize more than one language. In those countries, not everyone speaks more than one language, although bilingualism is obviously valuable. In fact, in some countries relatively few people speak the official language of the country. Those places generally have a small, powerful, wealthy elite and a large group of people who are disenfranchised.

National entities may choose an official language for practical rather than political reasons: Selecting a prevailing lingua franca is often convenient. But choosing one local language over another can provoke dissent and even rebellion. In those situations, a colonial lingua franca may prevail for political reasons. For example, in Africa, where national boundaries were historically determined by outside, colonial powers, countries may have multiple ethnicities and languages within their borders. Upon gaining independence, several of those countries adopted a prevailing colonial language such as English or French as their official language. Others have chosen a language that does not carry the baggage of colonial imposition.

The Rights of Language Minorities

Neither the United States as a whole nor individual states have a uniform, overarching language policy. Huebner (1999) points out that we have little in the way of explicit language policy, but attitudes, values, and beliefs have powerful effects on language practice in ways that are difficult to discern, study, or manipulate.

The role schools play in promoting or discouraging language inevitably embroils educators in the language debate, which usually takes the form of controversy about bilingual education. Nobody seems to doubt the value of bilingualism per se—people always claim they wish they spoke more than one language—but people object to offering education in languages other than English in the public schools. As we saw earlier, developing children's first languages in schools appears to support both second language acquisition and academic success. But that's a pedagogical argument that rarely carries much weight in the political debate, which is generally informed by emotion, popular belief, and the political issues of the day.

Ironically, even as people resist the notion of education in two languages, the need for people with language skills has grown. For example, following the events of September 11, 2001, federal agencies advertised on bilingual education e-mail lists for speakers of Arabic and other Middle Eastern languages, and universities scrambled to offer classes in Pashto, a language spoken in Afghanistan (Arnone, 2001).

The debate about the value of first language instruction for English language learners shows no sign of abating in the near future. As they plan instruction for language minority students, teachers need to be aware of the rights of language minorities.

Federal Policy and Second Language Learners

No federal laws mandate bilingual education. However, legislation does provide funding and support for services to English language learners. In addition, federal court decisions, focused primarily on civil rights for non-English speakers, support an entitlement to services that offer equal educational access to English language learners.

Title VII: The Bilingual Education Act

Signed into law in 1968, Title VII of the Elementary and Secondary Education Act (ESEA), known as the Bilingual Education Act, provided funds for direct services to students, teacher preparation, and support services such as technical assistance and dissemination of information. The act has been reauthorized many times since 1968, and both the level of funding and the emphases in the legislation have changed with each reauthorization.

Reauthorization in 2002: No Child Left Behind

The most recent reauthorization of the act, in 2002, is the "No Child Left Behind Act." The reauthorization signals changes in federal policy regarding the education of second language learners. The new policy direction is clearly signaled: The National Clearinghouse for Bilingual Education has been renamed the National Clearinghouse for English Language Acquisition and Language Instruction Educational Programs (NCELA). Also, the federal Office of Bilingual Education and Minority Language Affairs has been redesignated the Office of English Language Acquisition, Language Enhancement and Academic Achievement for Limited English Proficient Students.

Beyond labels, the act moves federal educational policy in the direction of local control. Until the recent reauthorization, funds available under the Bilingual Education Act were discretionary; that is, they were not automatically available to every student assessed as limited English proficient. Funds were awarded to state and local educational agencies, universities, and other educational institutions through a competitive proposal writing process. Under current legislation, in fiscal years where appropriations are less than $650 million, awards will be competitive. When funds exceed that amount, formula-based allocations will be made to states and state agencies will award subgrants. According to Crawford (2002), the new legislation appears to increase total resources for second language learners and serves more children, but at a lower allotment per child.

Although Title VII has never mandated bilingual education, it has effectively established policy at the national level through its acknowledgment of the needs of second language learners, its programmatic and instructional emphases, and its requirement that 75 percent of the act's funding be allotted to programs that support children's native language. There is no doubt that the new version of the act will radically alter the way we school second language learners.

Lau v. Nichols

The federal government has also had an impact on the education of second language learners through the courts. A discussion of the impact of the judicial system on education for second language learners must include the landmark U.S. Supreme Court decision in *Lau v. Nichols* (1974). It should be noted, however, that although *Lau* is important from a historical perspective, it no longer has any practical significance.

In 1974 a group of Chinese students sued the San Francisco Unified School District, claiming they were denied access to a meaningful education because they could not understand the education they received. They claimed the district violated Title VI of the Civil Rights Act of 1964, which prohibits discrimination on the basis of race, color, or national origin.

The Court found for the plaintiffs, but it didn't specify a remedy. As Piatt (1990) noted, *Lau* did not establish a constitutional right to bilingual education or even a requirement that districts provide primary-language content instruction.

Lau was, however, an important catalyst for public policy. Following the decision, the Department of Health, Education and Welfare of the federal government promulgated regulations regarding the identification of LEP students and the delivery of services to them. Although the regulations were never formally adopted, they were used as a de facto guide to *Lau* compliance by school districts and consequently had a far-reaching effect on programming for LEP students nationwide. After *Lau*, several states adopted legislation-mandating services for LEP students and New York City entered into a consent decree in *Aspira of New York v. Board of Education of the City of New York*, significantly expanding services to its large number of second language learners.

The Equal Educational Opportunities Act

Since *Lau v. Nichols*, various court decisions have reshaped judicial interpretation of Title VI of the Civil Rights Act (Crawford, 1989) and have mitigated the power of *Lau* as a protection for LEP students. Nevertheless, federal legislation has replaced *Lau* to some extent. Section 1703(f) of the Equal Educational Opportunities Act (EEOA) of 1974 states:

No State shall deny equal educational opportunity to an individual on account of his or her race, color, sex, or national origin by . . . (f) the failure by an educational agency to take appropriate action to overcome language barriers that impede equal participation by its students in its instructional programs.

The EEOA does not further elaborate on the rights of LEP students. The meaning of Section 1703(f) has been derived, therefore, from judicial interpretation, which has focused on the phrase "appropriate action."

What must school districts do to protect the rights afforded to LEP students by the EEOA? The standard for complying with the legislation has evolved from several court cases including *Castañeda v. Pickard* (1981); *Idaho Migrant Council v. Board of Education* (1981); *Keyes v. School District No. 1* (1983); and *Gomez v. Illinois State Board of Education* (1987). The basic requirement that derives from these cases is that LEP students must have equal access to the curriculum. "Appropriate action" as interpreted by federal courts includes

➤ A program based on sound educational theory,
➤ The allocation of trained personnel and material resources necessary to implement the program, and
➤ An evaluation and feedback process.

Equal access to the curriculum as defined by the courts does not require bilingual programs. Equal access does, however, prohibit districts from placing students in classrooms where they simply do not know what is going on. A careful reading of federal case law would suggest that districts should provide LEP students with a program that

➤ Addresses the development of English language skills; and

➤ Assures that LEP students do not learn less because of their lack of knowledge of English.

State Law

In the 1970s, following *Lau*, many states passed legislation mandating services to LEP students. In the 1980s, however, as federal support for bilingual education became more uncertain, several states, including California and Colorado, eliminated their mandates for bilingual education. More recently, California passed an initiative that eliminates bilingual education except in cases where parents affirmatively request programs. Similar initiatives are gaining support in other states, fueled by fear of immigration and persistent American nativism that inevitably lead to support for English-only movements.

World events, changes in federal policy, and renewed debates about immigration and immigrants' rights assure continued debate about the use of languages other than English in the public schools.

References

Arnone, M. (2001, December 21). Colleges scramble to offer online courses in Pashto. *Chronicle of Higher Education*, p. A27.

Aspira of New York v. Board of Education of the City of New York, Civ. No. 4002 (S.D.NY. consent agreement, August 29, 1974).

Castañeda v. Pickard, 64 F.2d 989 (5th Cir. 1981).

Crawford, J. (1989). *Bilingual education: History, politics, theory, and practice*. Trenton, NJ: Crane Publishing.

Crawford, J. (1992). *Hold your tongue: Bilingualism and the politics of English only*. Reading, MA: Addison-Wesley.

Crawford, J. (2002). Obituary: The Bilingual Education Act, 1968–2002. [Online]. Available: Ourworld.compuserve.com/hompages/JWCRA FORD/home.htm. Spring 2002.

Giroux, H. (1988). *Teachers as intellectuals: Toward a critical pedagogy of Learning*. Granby, MA: Bergin & Garvey.

Gomez v. Illinois State Board of Education, 811 F.2d 1030 (7th Cir. 1987).

Huebner, T. (1999). Sociopolitical perspectives on language policy, politics, and praxis. In T. Huebner & K. A. Davis (Eds.), *Sociopolitical perspectives on language policy and planning in the USA* (pp. 1–15). Philadelphia: John Benjamins.

Idaho Migrant Council v. Board of Education, 647 F.2d 69 (9th Cir. 1981).

Keys v. School District No. 1, Denver, Colorado, 576 F. Supp. 1503 (D. Colo. 1983).

Lau v. Nichols, 414 U.S. 563 (1974).

Mercury News Wire Services (2002, January 23). Turkey: 17 Kurdish students jailed over petition. *San Jose Mercury News*, p. 7A. *Meyer v. Nebraska*, 262 U.S. 390 (1923).

Piatt, B. (1990). *Only English? Law and language policy in the United States*. Albuquerque: University of New Mexico Press.

Thomas, R. M., Jr. (1998, February 1). Carl Gorman, Code talker in World War II, dies at 90. *New York Times*, p. 31.

▲ ▲ ▲

Read More About . . .

➤ Navajo code talkers in *The Unbreakable Code,* by Sara Hoagland Hunter (Flagstaff, AZ: Northland, 1996). This is a children's book, beautifully written and illustrated, and certainly suitable for young readers, but equally appealing and informative for adults.

➤ What happens to the languages of immigrants to the United States in two new books: *"Why Don't They Learn English?": Separating Fact from Fallacy in the U.S. Language Debate,* by Lucy Tse (New York: Teachers College Press, 2001), and *Legacies: The Story of the Immigrant Second Generation,* by Alejandro Portes and Ruben Rumbaut (Berkeley: University of California Press, 2001).

➤ The loss of the world's languages in *Language Death,* by David Crystal (New York: Cambridge University Press, 2000). Another scholarly book on the same topic is *Vanishing Voices: The Extinction of the World's Languages,* by Daniel Nettle and Suzanne Romaine (New York: Oxford University Press, 2000). Everything you might want to know about the world's languages, minority language rights, language loss, the role of schools in *Linguistic Genocide in Education, or Worldwide Diversity and Human Rights?* by Tove Skutnabb-Kangas (L. Erlbaum, 2000). Skutnabb-Kangas is one of the most original thinkers and respected scholars in the field of language policy and planning. This book is an encyclopedic compilation of information about language. It is also a powerful analysis of the way globalization destroys the culture and languages of the world's indigenous peoples and how that is an indescribable loss for us all.

➤ The nature and impact of shortages of speakers of foreign language on important federal agencies, including the U.S. Army, the Department of State, the Department of Commerce, and the Federal Bureau of Education, in *Foreign Languages: Human Capital Approach Needed to Correct Staffing and Proficiency Shortfalls.* The report, published in 2002, is available from the U.S. General Accounting Office (GAO-02-375).

➤ Readers may want to check the new Web site on language policy research recently developed by the Education Policy Studies Laboratory at Arizona State University. The site is located at www.language-policy.org.

▲   ▲   ▲

6

FREQUENTLY ASKED
QUESTIONS ABOUT LANGUAGE
TEACHING AND LEARNING

PEOPLE HAVE POWERFUL EMOTIONAL RESPONSES TO LANGUAGE AND culture and strong opinions about public education. Questions about how best to meet the needs of second language learners are often provocative. This book has attempted to present a cool, even-handed look at some of the issues involved. What follows are some of the more frequently asked questions about language teaching and learning. Some answers may recapitulate material presented earlier, but they are included for review and emphasis. Also included are additional resources for readers who want to pursue issues in further depth.

I don't speak a language other than English, and anyway the students in my classroom speak several different primary languages. What strategies can I use to help them?

Academic instruction can be modified in several ways to make the content accessible to second language learners. All teachers should do the following:

➤ Create a predictable classroom environment. Establishing routines, marking transitions between activities, and using clear signals assist second language learners in understanding expectations. Consistent routines help learners make connections between activities and the language that accompanies them.

➤ Build academic language skills. Teachers usually identify new and important vocabulary for all students. Second language learners may also need help with process vocabulary. Words such as *list, compare, describe,* or *explain* may be unfamiliar and should be reviewed for students working in a new language.

➤ Provide context for activities. Use visuals and hands-on activities whenever possible to help provide comprehensible language input.

➤ Use questions effectively. Be sure to leave enough time for a response because second language learners may need more time than native speakers to answer a question. Listen for meaning in their answers, rather than correctness of speech, and acknowledge correct content. Repeat students' answers and paraphrase them if necessary to model correct language forms. Provide opportunities for nonverbal responses to questions: For example, ask students to indicate a response on a map, a chart, or a graph.

➤ Facilitate understanding. Check your comprehension of what a student says. If necessary, repeat and rephrase questions and answers. Listen for communication, not correctness. Constant correction stifles communication. When communication is emphasized, students will feel comfortable, generate language, and receive language input, all of which supports language development.

Language is an important component of instruction and modifying language can ease the experience of a student working in a new language. Other important considerations come into play, however, in classrooms characterized by diversity. California Tomorrow publishes excellent resources for responding to the needs of diverse student populations. Educators can access the organization's Web site at www.californiatomorrow.org.

What is a newcomer program?
Imagine you are a teenager who has come from a country where few people attend school past the early grades. You don't speak English, and you have never been in a high school, much less an American high school, until the day you find yourself in one. Bells ring, announcements are made over the public announcement system, crowds of students move through the halls—you haven't the faintest idea where to go, what to do, or what's expected of you—an overwhelming, even frightening experience.

Newcomer programs place immigrant students in special

academic programs designed to facilitate their transition into American schools. Such programs may provide some academic content instruction as well as high intensity English instruction, and they also usually help students and their families understand how the American school system works. The Center for Applied Linguistics has published an overview of newcomer programs on its Web site. The study, funded by the Center for Research on Education, Diversity, and Excellence, is available at www.cal.org/crede/newcomer. htm.

What is the best age to learn a second language?

People generally assume that children learn a second language faster and better than adults do. The idea of a *critical period* prior to puberty has some support among psycholinguists, but current thinking suggests that, though very young children can simultaneously learn two or more languages as *first* languages, older children and adults can learn second languages quite well.

The obvious difference between youngsters and older learners is that children seem to readily acquire a nativelike accent that most adults find difficult to attain. This may be partly because of the neurological maturation process of brain *lateralization,* which seems to limit the plasticity of the brain. Another possible explanation is that children have better psychomotor skills than adults, and those skills help them master the phonological system of a language.

In any event, mastery of the phonological system is not necessary for language proficiency. H. Douglas Brown, whose book *Principles of Language Learning and Teaching* (1987) is a classic in the field, makes the following observation:

> Pronunciation of a language is not by any means the sole criterion for acquisition, nor is it really the most important one. We all know people who have less than perfect pronunciation but who also have magnificent and fluent control of a second language, control that can even exceed that of many native speakers. I like to call this the 'Henry Kissinger' effect in honor of the former U.S. Secretary of State whose German accent was so noticeable yet who was clearly more eloquent than the large majority of native speakers of American English (pp. 46–67).

Although age may have some bearing on the ability to learn a second language, other factors come into play as well. For example, personality may play a role. Extroverted, confident people are more likely to attempt communication in a new language and thereby generate the language input that seems to facilitate learning. Motivation is also a factor. An individual may be motivated, for example, to learn a new language if it will result in career advancement. Cultural factors, attitudes, and biases may affect a person's motivation to learn a second language. In many places in the world, bilingualism is the norm, and people learn more than one language without much fanfare—indeed without schooling.

We speak two languages at home. How can we raise a bilingual child?

Studies of early acquisition of more than one language are not numerous. They are often case studies done by psycholinguists making observations of their own children. As such, they may be somewhat unsystematic and may be biased. It is clear, however, that around the world, many children are raised "bilingual as a first language."

Following are four common strategies that people use when they want to raise bilingual children:

➤ One person, one language, or separation of language by person.

➤ Minority language in the home, majority language outside, or separation of language by place.

➤ Language separated by time or situation, for example, one language in the morning, another in the afternoon.

➤ One language initially, and a second between the ages of three and five.

(Grosjean, 1982)

"One person, one language" is probably the most common approach that parents take. Any approach, however, is subject to the effects of a child's sociolinguistic environment. A child who learns a low-status language may have difficulty maintaining that language once schooling starts. Parents who are highly motivated to maintain their home language should seek out additive bilingual programs for their children and provide opportunities for their child to develop literacy in their home language.

What are the rights of undocumented students?
In 1982, the U.S. Supreme Court ruled in *Plyler v. Doe,* 457 U.S. 202, that, under the Equal Protection Clause of the 14th Amendment, public schools cannot deny children access to public education based on the children's immigration status. Specifically, schools may not do the following:

➤ Bar a student from school on the basis of immigration status.

➤ Classify a student as a nonresident based on undocumented status.

➤ Inquire about a students' immigration status.

➤ Make inquiries of a student or parents, which might expose their undocumented status.

➤ Require the social security numbers of all students.

The National Coalition of Advocates for Students is an excellent resource for information about the rights and needs of immigrant students and effective strategies for addressing their needs. Information about their publications is available on the Web at www.neasboston.org.

Should the United States have an official language policy?
All over the world, knowledge of English is considered essential. The majority of English speakers in the world have

learned it as a second language for scholarship, business, and diplomacy. In the United States everyone—including immigrants, refugees, and indigenous minorities—is aware of the need to learn English. English is neither dead nor dying, as is usually the case with a language whose speakers feel the need for protective legislation. What then motivates us to consider mandating English as our official language?

U.S. English, the group spearheading the movement, is a spin-off of the efforts of the Federation for American Immigration Reform, whose agenda has been to limit immigration. Immigration has been a constant in U.S. history and has invariably been accompanied by nativist movements. Such reactionary movements have left us the embarrassing legacy of the Know-Nothing movement, which tried to exclude Irish Catholics from holding public office; the Chinese Exclusion Act, which halted immigration from China; and the Barred Zone Act, which prohibited Asians from obtaining citizenship—to cite just a few examples.

Our national immigration policy changed in 1965, and we now admit equal numbers of people from every country in the world, with exceptions for some people who are granted special refugee status. The diversity of newcomers heightens their presence in our minds and excites our xenophobia, provoking us to nativist thinking manifested in the English-only movement.

An enforced English-only policy would limit programs such as court translations, translation assistance in hospitals, and other related public services for those who require them. It would eliminate bilingual balloting, which expands citizens' access to the political process and benefits all of us by strengthening the democratic process.

An English-only policy would not, however, miraculously result in a nation of English speakers. People tend to learn the languages they need to succeed in daily life and to resist the languages imposed on them. Our societal energy would be best directed toward providing English as a second language classes for the many adults who are on waiting lists at our night schools and community colleges. English maintains its status in the United States without forcible imposition.

James Crawford, an independent writer and former editor of *Education Week,* is probably the leading expert on U.S. language policy and the English-only movement. Educators will want to read his most recent book, *At War with Diversity: U.S. Language Policy in an Age of Anxiety* (Buffalo, NY: Multilingual Matters, 2000), as well as his other books: *Bilingual Education: History, Politics, Theory, and Practice* (Los Angeles: Bilingual Education Service, 1995); *Hold Your Tongue: Bilingualism and the Politics of English Only* (Reading, MA: Addison-Wesley, 1992); and *Language Loyalties: A Source Book on the Official English Controversy* (Chicago: University of Chicago Press, 1992). Information about these publications and other valuable information are available on his Web site, ourworld.compuserve.com/homepages/JWCRAWFORD/.

Why is bilingual education a politically charged issue?
People who are opposed to bilingual education are usually not opposed to bilingualism per se, but they feel strongly

that primary language instruction should not be made available to language minority students who are learning English as a second language. This opposition exists despite ample evidence that primary language instruction improves the academic performance of students who have not mastered English well enough to function in English-only classrooms. There is also ample evidence that public policy support for bilingualism would be economically, politically, and strategically beneficial for us as a nation. Nevertheless, opposition to bilingual education continues and has even intensified in the last decade.

To understand the nature of this opposition, we must travel beyond pedagogical boundaries and enter the world of political considerations. One scholar (Moran, 1987) has suggested that minority support and mainstream opposition both stem from the recognition that publicly funded bilingual programs represent public support for languages other than English and, by extension, the cultures and values that they embody.

Cummins elaborated on this perspective in *Empowering Minority Students* (Sacramento, CA: California Association for Bilingual Education, 1989), in which he suggests that "the fear that has engendered such a negative reaction to bilingual education is the fear of social change, of minority empowerment" (pp. 109–110). Bilingual programs do, in fact, seek to empower minority populations by doing the following:

➤ Making schools accessible to parents in a language they understand;

➤ Providing an instructional curriculum that is reflective of, and responsive to, the minority groups in a particular community; and

➤ Giving second language learners equal access to the curriculum.

Who should receive a bilingual education?
Everyone.

References

Brown, H.D. (1987). *Principles of language learning and teaching.* Englewood Cliffs, NJ: Prentice-Hall.

Cummins J. (1989). *Empowering minority students.* Sacramento, CA: California Association for Bilingual Education.

Grosjean, F. (1982*). Life with two languages: An introduction to bilingualism.* Cambridge, MA: Harvard University Press.

Moran, R. (1987). Bilingual education as a status conflict. *California law review* 75: 321–361.

ABBREVIATIONS

BICS	Basic Interpersonal Communicative Skills
CALP	Cognitive Academic Language Proficiency
EEOA	Equal Educational Opportunities Act
ELD	English Language Development
ELL	English Language Learners
ESEA	Elementary and Secondary Education Act
ESL	English as a Second Language
LAD	Language Acquisition Device
LEP	Limited English Proficient
NCELA	National Clearinghouse for English Language Acquisition and Language Instruction Educational Programs
OELA	Office of English Language Acquisition

INDEX

Note: Information in figures is indicated by an italic *f.*

ABOUT THE AUTHOR

JUDITH LESSOW-HURLEY IS A PROFESSOR IN THE ELEMENTARY Education Department at San José State University in San José, California. She taught in bilingual classrooms in New York and Colorado, and has been involved with professional development for teachers in California, Colorado, New York, and Texas, as well as abroad. Lessow-Hurley also worked with the National Board for Professional Teaching Standards and the California Commission on Teacher Credentialing to establish standards for teachers who work with second language learners. Her book *The Foundations of Dual Language Instruction* (3rd edition, Longman, 2000) is used in teacher preparation programs nationwide. In addition to her work in bilingual education, Lessow-Hurley has taught courses in multicultural education and has been involved in research and program development related to religious diversity and public schooling.

You may contact the author by mail at San José State University, College of Education, Elementary Education Department, San José, California 95192-0074, or by e-mail at judithlh@email.sjsu.edu.